jenni kayne

Pacific
Natural

Jenni Kayne

Pacific Natural

Simple Seasonal Entertaining

Foreword by Martha Stewart

New York · Paris · London · Milan

CONTENTS

FOREWORD

by Martha Stewart

Jenni Kayne is the personification of Pacific Natural, the subject of her beautiful book of the same name. As a working woman, wife, mother, designer, entrepreneur, and now author, Jenni lives the life she so passionately espouses in this wonderfully photographed, stylishly conceived book. This is a lifestyle we would all be happy to adopt.

Jenni's aesthetic is indicative of the casual but elegant, healthy but fashionable approach she displays in everything she does. Her cooking is simple but sophisticated, her decor is understated but of the moment, the outdoors are her indoors, and her tablescapes are always quietly evocative of her surroundings.

This book invites us into Jenni's world and takes us where we would all like to be, serving us images of foods we would all love to make and eat, encouraging and reminding us that celebrating with family and our friends is always an occasion.

INTRODUCTION

There is nothing I love more than bringing people together. I find that sharing a table is the most meaningful way to connect with people, whether they be old friends, new friends, or family. My grandmother, Ida, was known to bring in stray kids from the neighborhood and host them at her dinner table. I like to think that my love of entertaining comes from her.

This book is a glimpse into how I make every occasion, big or small, a special one. Entertaining isn't about chasing perfection. It's about creating beautiful moments with the people that surround you. For most of us, life is busy and often complicated, but much fuller and richer when shared with those you love. This book is here to inspire you to make memories in your own way, wherever you may be, with whomever you choose.

As the seasons change in California, the nature of each gathering changes. From an outdoor picnic to a cozy brunch, I try to keep each occasion sensitive to the beauty that surrounds us. Eating seasonally isn't just good for us, it also helps us be aware of the world and to appreciate all of its gifts.

You'll find this book broken up into seasons, with a menu that includes a parting gift for your guests, my tips for the table, and a seasonal craft.

From the valley of Ojai to the ranches of Santa Ynez, the shores of Lake Tahoe, and to home in Los Angeles, these are the places that are near and dear to my heart. This is where I find my inspiration. This is the landscape that shapes the memories I look back on and the traditions I look forward to.

Living well is as much about fresh air and good food as it is about coming together with those we love. Entertaining is my way of taking time to slow things down, appreciate my natural surroundings, express gratitude, and feel connected to the world around me. I hope this inspires you to do the same.

XX Jenni

Elements of Entertaining

Entertaining is just as much about creating a good time for others as it is about enjoying yourself. A successful dinner party is all about the prep work: having a few basic tricks up my sleeve makes everything fall into place. That's why I love a theme, because all the little details are what make an event truly memorable. Each party might have its own style, but they all speak the same language. Throughout these chapters, you'll see how I set the table with respect to each season or occasion, focusing on certain elements to bring it all together, from decor to dessert.

Event Checklist

☑ MENU

☑ SIGNATURE COCKTAIL

☑ TABLE SETTING

☑ FLORALS

☑ PARTING GIFT

Supply Closet

LINENS

*Layers of neutral hues sit well on any table.
Consider a runner, a set of 6-12 napkins, and a tablecloth.*

CANDLES

*Candles create an ambiance with low lighting. Don't forget to
protect surfaces from drips of wax with candleholders or bases.*

POTTERY & CERAMICS

*Keep an eye out for those special pieces you'll love to display.
Use for flowers and as centerpieces.*

WOOD BOWLS

*These rustic vessels are great for serving or for decor filled
with fruit, veggies, florals, or a mixture of all three.*

WOOD BOARDS

Layer these full of appetizers like cheeses and crudités.

LEATHER CORD & JUTE TWINE

*Use to wrap gifts, as a napkin holder, or to tie herb
bundles and florals together.*

CARDSTOCK

*Add a personal touch with handwritten or
printed place cards, menus, and thank-you notes.*

GLASS JARS

*Gather a variety of shapes and sizes to gift,
craft, and store dry goods.*

LINEN & BURLAP

*Use to wrap gifts, as a drop cloth for craft tables,
and you can even make your own tablecloth or runner.*

GLASSWARE

*Keep a variety of glasses on hand that are versatile
enough to use for wine, water, or cocktails.*

PLATES, BOWLS, & CUTLERY

*Earthy neutrals let the food be the focus
and work for every occasion.*

CARAFES

*Help your guests help themselves by filling
with water or mixed drinks.*

FOLDING TABLES

*Quickly put together a table. Throw a nice linen
on top and your guests will never know the difference.*

Arranging Flowers

Filling your home with fresh flowers makes all the difference in the world. I love to bring the outside in, and fragrant blooms add that extra-special layer of decor in the home. I find the process of arranging florals themselves is quite meditative. I buy my flowers at the flower mart, at my local farmers market, or simply just forage florals and greens from my surroundings. Here are just a few basic guidelines to building your own arrangements and making them last.

Choose a vessel with an opening that will fit the blooms you're arranging. Clean and rinse to make sure it is clear of dirt or residue and fill with cool water.

—

Measure the desired height of your flowers by holding in front of the vessel before trimming stems to their proper length. Use clean, sharp floral shears and cut the ends of the stems on a diagonal.

—

For woodsy stems and branches, smash the ends. This will help them to absorb water.

Clean the stems by stripping away any leaves or thorns that will touch water. This keeps your water clean and makes flowers last longer.

—

There are a few tools you can use to help hold your flowers in place that you can find at your local craft store or flower shop. For vases with tall, wide openings, use a tape grid. For low, wide openings, use a flower frog. Rubber bands work for narrower openings to help hold your flowers exactly where you want them.

—

If placing your arrangement in an entryway, taller arrangements make a welcoming statement. For a dining table, lower florals are best so guests can see across the table. On small surfaces like a nightstand, coffee or console table, group bud vases together and use just one or two stems.

—

Create a base with greenery or choose fuller, larger blooms to place first. Next, insert stems that will add height or dimension. Lastly, add special flowers or greens that pop or add an accent to your arrangement.

—

Don't be afraid to cut off a branch or bloom if it's not working.

—

Add water every day and change the water every 2-3 days. For more delicate flowers like orchids, add two ice cubes for a slow drip of hydration to avoid overwatering.

< *Drop a penny into your vase. The copper will acidify the water and prevent fungus and bacteria from growing.*

What's In Season

Living in California means we have access to so much produce all year round, but enjoying a fruit or vegetable in its very prime brings a whole new dimension to a plate. Consider a tomato picked right off the vine in the height of summer. The bright and flavorful taste is far superior to a store-bought bunch in the off-season.

One of my favorite ways to find the freshest produce is by strolling through my local farmers market and asking vendors what's in season and what they recommend. Even better, plant your own garden. This can seem intimidating at first, but there are some low-maintenance, no-fuss seeds that will thrive under many conditions. Start out with some common kitchen herbs like rosemary, thyme, or cilantro.

Bringing in seasonal flowers and greens from the outdoors can really bring a table to life. In the upcoming chapters, you can see how I integrate flowers, herbs, fruits, and vegetable to complement a meal, make a craft, and decorate the house.

Here are the vegetables, fruits, and flowers I look forward to each and every season.

My friend Lauri Kranz's >
incredible edible garden.

Spring

Think fresh salads with raw, crunchy veggies, bitter greens, and the beginning of sweet berry season. Nothing says spring like blooms in vibrant colors.

VEGETABLES		FRUITS		FLOWERS	
Artichoke	*Green beans*	*Avocado*	*Lime*	*Anemone*	*Iris*
Asparagus	*Lettuce*	*Apricot*	*Mango*	*Daffodil*	*Lilac*
Carrots	*Radicchio*	*Bitter melon*	*Orange*	*Delphinium*	*Peony*
Chives	*Radish*	*Jackfruit*	*Raspberries*	*Fritillaria*	*Ranunculus*
Fennel	*Spinach*	*Lemon*	*Strawberries*	*Helleborus*	*Sweet pea*

Summer

Think juicy stone fruits, vibrant, jewel-toned berries, and bursts of bright, refreshing flavors.
Colorful wildflowers and sturdy perennials thrive in this season.

VEGETABLES

Arugula	Eggplant
Beet	Fava beans
Bell pepper	Okra
Corn	Summer squash
Cucumber	Zucchini

FRUITS

Avocado	Mulberries
Blueberries	Nectarine
Cherries	Peach
Fig	Plum
Melon	Tomato

FLOWERS

Coreopsis	Lisianthus
Dahlia	Scabiosa
Hydrangea	Strawflower
Garden rose	Sunflower
Lavender	Yarrow

Fall

Think earthy elements and root vegetables. Autumnal flowers come
in a spectrum of vibrant reds, yellows, and rusts.

VEGETABLES		FRUITS		FLOWERS	
Bell pepper	*Celery root*	*Apple*	*Passion fruit*	*Celosia*	*Marigold*
Broccoli	*Mushrooms*	*Grapes*	*Pear*	*Chrysanthemum*	*Ornamental corn*
Butternut squash	*Potato*	*Guava*	*Persimmon*	*Dahlias*	*Pansy*
Cabbage	*Pumpkin*	*Huckleberries*	*Pomegranate*	*Dianthus*	*Rudbeckia*
Cauliflower	*Squash*	*Key lime*	*Quince*	*Herbs*	*Strawflower*

Winter

Think deep, saturated hues, dark leafy greens, and tart citrus. Evergreen arrangements
can brave the cold to accompany more ornamental flowers.

VEGETABLES		FRUITS		FLOWERS	
Beet	*Onion*	*Blood orange*	*Kiwi*	*Algerian iris*	*Pine*
Carrots	*Parsnip*	*Clementine*	*Mandarin orange*	*Calendula*	*Primrose*
Celery	*Potato*	*Cranberries*	*Papaya*	*Cedar*	*Snowdrop*
Kale	*Pumpkin*	*Dates*	*Star fruit*	*Echinacea*	*Spruce*
Leeks	*Swiss chard*	*Grapefruit*	*Tangerine*	*Icelandic poppy*	*Winter jasmine*

Appetizers

Setting out a simple cheese board or crudité plate is one of my favorite party tricks. If your dinner takes longer to prep, a plate of farm-fresh veggies and an array of interesting cheeses will hold your guests over while you're tending to the finishing touches in the kitchen. The success of the snack plate relies on the combinations you put together. Go for a mix of color and texture, and don't worry about making it look too perfect.

Cheese Board

Start with a simple, smooth surface like wood, marble, or ceramic.

—

Choose a variety of three to five cheeses. A good rule of thumb is
to portion out about three ounces of cheese per person.

—

Put faith in your local cheese shop. They can recommend the
perfect cheeses based on what you're serving alongside them.

—

Pick a few cheeses you know and like,
and add in some new varieties you want to try,
mixing soft and hard cheeses.

< Arrange complementary flavors in groups. Mix salty with sweet and play with height—feel free to really pile it on.

Here's a good starting point:

Goat cheese

Cheddar cheese

Camembert

Parmigiano-Reggiano

—

Let the cheese sit at room temperature for 30 minutes
before serving.

—

While the cheese softens, assemble your ingredients.

—

Throw in a few nuts, olives, and fresh or dried fruits.

—

Make sure you have the right utensils on hand and cut a few slices
for your guests to get them started. Don't forget
bowls for pits and shells.

Crudité Board

Prepare by cutting up your preferred ingredients two hours in
advance so your vegetables stay fresh and crisp.

—

Choose a variety of complementary colors to make your
presentation as eye-catching as possible.

Here are a few suggestions:

Watermelon radishes

Green beans

Cherry tomatoes

Rainbow carrots

Sugar snap peas

< *Blanching brings out
vibrant texture and
color in veggies like
green beans, snap peas,
and broccoli. Boil salted
water and blanch each
type separately, 2-5
minutes, then shock in an
ice bath before plating.*

—

Experiment with different methods of cutting and peeling
your veggies. The more undone, the better.

—

Set out a couple of dips alongside your board. Some of my favorites
are hummus and green goddess dressing.

Spring

SPRING IN OJAI

A Rosemary Dinner

A Citrus Lunch

A Floral Garden Party

Lavender Body Oil

Dried Herbs

Spring is a time of new life and new beginnings. Wildflowers begin to bloom and sunny days look forward to the summer ahead. We eat our veggies raw, making the most of the season's bounty, and welcome the energy of change that's in the air.

I love Ojai for its beauty, serenity, and opportunities to enjoy the outdoors. Arranging dinner around a single ingredient brings us closer to our surroundings, grounded amongst acres of citrus groves and orchards. In the following pages, I'll show you how to dry herbs you can use all year round, make an aromatic spray to gift your guests, and celebrate this buoyant season with simple crafts and recipes.

A ROSEMARY DINNER

Earthy and bright, rosemary acts as both ingredient and ornament. This herb is truly one of my favorites, for the way it affects the senses with its savory taste and powerful fragrance, and its versatility. It's beautiful both on the table and on the plate. I am always inspired by the landscape around me and I love to make the most of the plants growing in my garden. Aromatic and evergreen, rosemary infuses every detail of this dinner, from the lush, effortlessly undone centerpieces, to the sprigs tied to linen napkins, to the light bites and thoughtful parting gifts.

Rosemary Paloma

To make the rosemary agave syrup: Combine blue agave, water, and rosemary in a saucepan over medium heat. Simmer for 5 minutes. Remove from heat and let cool. Strain cooled mixture through a mesh strainer. Discard rosemary and use immediately. Store excess in an airtight container and refrigerate for up to 2 weeks.

To make the paloma: Combine tequila, grapefruit juice, lime juice, and rosemary agave syrup in a large pitcher and stir. Divide evenly between 6 ice-filled glasses. Garnish each cocktail with a sprig of rosemary and a slice of citrus.

INGREDIENTS

Serves 6

Rosemary Agave Syrup

½ cup blue agave

½ cup water

3 sprigs rosemary

Paloma

2 cups blanco tequila

1 cup freshly squeezed grapefruit juice

1 cup freshly squeezed lime juice

¾ cup rosemary agave syrup

Rosemary sprigs, for garnish

Lime or grapefruit, sliced, for garnish

Grapefruit peels, for garnish

Crostini with Ricotta, Wild Mushroom & Rosemary

INGREDIENTS

Serves 6

1 sourdough baguette

3 tablespoons olive oil, plus more for drizzling

Salt & black pepper

1 pound mixed mushrooms, torn into pieces

1 shallot, minced

1 clove garlic, minced

1 teaspoon fresh thyme

1 tablespoon rosemary, minced

2 tablespoons sherry vinegar

1 pint fresh ricotta

Chopped rosemary or parsley,

for garnish

To make the crostini: Heat oven to 375° F. Line a baking sheet with parchment paper and set aside. With a serrated knife, cut the baguette into ¼-inch slices. Arrange the baguette slices in a single layer on the baking sheet. Drizzle with olive oil, season with salt and pepper. Bake for 6-7 minutes, until crostini are crisp and golden brown at the edges.

To prepare the mushrooms: Heat a large sauté pan with 1 tablespoon olive oil over medium heat. When the oil begins to shimmer, add mushrooms and a generous pinch of salt. Stir every so often about 8-10 minutes, until the mushrooms begin to soften and get a bit of color. Push the mushrooms to one side of the pan. On the opposite side of the pan, add the 3 tablespoons olive oil and add the shallot, garlic, thyme, and rosemary. Toast for 1-2 minutes. Combine with the mushrooms and continue cooking for another 5 minutes.

Turn off the heat and carefully pour in the sherry vinegar to deglaze the pan. Scrape the bottom with a wooden spoon as the liquid comes to a boil and let cool.

To assemble the crostini: Line the baked crostini on a platter and smear with a dollop of ricotta, then top with a tablespoon of the cooked mushrooms. Garnish with fresh rosemary or parsley and salt and pepper to taste.

Tips for the Table

*Use herbs from the garden as an arrangement to
complement the herbs in your meal.*

—

*Sheepskins over benches or chairs are
cozy and textural, and add a little comfort
for your guests.*

—

*Mini baguettes make a great table setting.
Wrap some twine and fabric around each loaf and
attach place cards.*

—

*Seating arrangements aren't meant to be confining,
they are simply a way to facilitate conversation
and introduce people to one another.*

—

*Play with varying heights of tapered candles
to add a bit of dimension to the table.*

—

*Instead of playing bartender all night, encourage
guests to mix their own beverages. Offer them their
first drink and then lead them to the cocktail table,
set up with ingredients and instructions.*

Parting Gift | Rosemary Spray

SUPPLIES

Makes 1 bottle

2 ounces water

18 drops rosemary essential oil

2-ounce glass spray bottle

Sprig of fresh rosemary

I love to refresh a room with a spritz of rosemary spray. The herbal scent is perfect for the kitchen or bathroom, but you can experiment with your favorite essential oils to find a scent you love.

To make one bottle of rosemary spray: Combine water with rosemary essential oil in the glass bottle. To gift, add the sprig of rosemary inside the bottle or attach it to the bottle with twine. Remove the sprig before use.

A CITRUS LUNCH

Ojai is renowned for its stunning sunsets, wellness retreats, and miles of winding citrus orchards. From March to May, harvest season sees a bounty of the valley's signature pixies, along with plenty of oranges, lemons, and grapefruits. When these bright and zesty fruits are abundant, I incorporate them everywhere. I love pairing citrus with flavors both savory and sweet, leaving them whole or cut in half on the table as decor, and using the bright aroma in crafts around the home.

Kale & Blood Orange Salad

To roast the beets: Heat oven to 425° F. Combine beets, oil and salt and toss to coat. Place beets in a baking dish with water and orange juice, and cover with aluminum oil. Roast 45 minutes to 1 hour, until a fork can easily penetrate the center of the beet. Set aside until cool to the touch. Use a paper towel to gently remove the skin. Slice or dice.

To make the vinaigrette: Combine lemon juice, blood orange juice, Dijon mustard, salt, pepper, and red chili flakes in a blender. With the blender running, pour the olive oil in a slow, steady stream until thoroughly mixed. Season to taste.

To assemble the salad: Massage kale with the dressing, reserving some for the beets. Salt and pepper to taste. Add the blood oranges. Drizzle the remaining dressing on the cooked beets. Place the dressed kale and citrus into a serving dish and layer in beets, pistachios and feta. Finish with salt and pepper.

INGREDIENTS

Serves 6

Roasted Beets

1 ½ pound beets, tops cut off, skin on

2 tablespoons grapeseed or olive oil

Salt

1 cup water

½ cup freshly squeezed orange juice

Citrus Vinaigrette

2 tablespoons freshly squeezed lemon juice

2 tablespoons freshly squeezed blood orange juice

2 tablespoons Dijon mustard

Pinch of salt

Pinch of black pepper

Pinch of red chili flakes

1 cup olive oil

Kale Salad

3 bunches kale, stemmed & torn

4 blood oranges, rinds removed, sliced, & quartered

¾ cup pistachios, coarsely chopped & toasted

¾ cup French feta, crumbled

Naked Kumquat Cake

Vanilla Cake

4 cups rice flour

4 cups gluten-free flour

1⅓ cup almond flour

4 tablespoons plus 1 teaspoon baking powder

2 tablespoons salt

24 egg whites

4 tablespoons vanilla bean paste or pure vanilla extract

6 cups sugar

1 cup plus 2 tablespoons grapeseed oil

5 cups milk

20 ounces unsalted butter, melted

Cream Cheese Frosting

24 ounces cream cheese, room temperature

½ pound (2 sticks) unsalted butter, room temperature

2 teaspoons vanilla extract

4½ cups confectioners' sugar

Toppings

10 kumquats cut into rounds, seeds removed

Handful whole & halved kumquats

Citrus leaves

To make the cake: Heat oven to 350° F. Prepare four (9-inch round) cake pans by greasing with butter or oil. Line with parchment paper and set aside. In a mixing bowl, combine flours, baking powder, and salt. Separately, in a large mixing bowl, mix egg whites, vanilla, and sugar until fully dissolved. Add oil and stir to combine. Add milk and stir until fully combined. Gently add the flour mixture to the egg mixture and stir to combine. Add butter and stir until combined. Divide the cake batter evenly between the four cake pans. Bake for 22-25 minutes, until a toothpick inserted into the center of the cake comes out clean. Let the cakes fully cool on wire racks before removing them from the pans.

To make the frosting: Beat cream cheese in a stand mixer. Add butter and vanilla. Beat until smooth. Add powdered sugar and beat until smooth.

To build the cake: Place a 9-inch cake board on a turntable cake stand and add one layer of cake. Top with a cup of frosting and smooth over the top of cake. Repeat with each layer of cake. Leave the sides of the cake naked or add a few smears of frosting—whatever suits your style. Decorate liberally with kumquats, citrus leaves, or tailor to fit the inspiration for the occasion.

Tips for the Table

*Use whole and halved fruits alongside florals.
Light, delicate blooms complement the aroma of
citrus perfectly.*

—

*Wooden bowls are a great alternative to vases. Fill
them with fruits, vegetables, or cut greens at the
center of the table.*

—

*Natural linen still looks pretty when it's a bit
wrinkled; just add a piece of leather twine around
a rolled-up napkin for each place setting.*

—

*Play with the height and width of your cake.
You could even make mini cakes and have each
guest decorate one—it's a great way to interact and
fun to see everyone express themselves.*

—

*Change things up and find a unique
place to eat. Have friends help move the table
outside for a change of scenery.*

Parting Gift | Citrus Bath Salts

Scoop citrus salts into a warm bath and enjoy the uplifting aroma of lemon and orange zest to ease the mind and relax the body.

To make a jar of bath salts: In a glass jar, combine epsom salt, sea salt, and baking soda with a few drops each of essential oil and the citrus zest. Mix well and seal tight.

SUPPLIES

Makes 1 jar

3-ounce glass jar with cork top

1½ cup epsom salt

¾ cup sea salt

¼ cup baking soda

Lemon & orange essential oils

1 teaspoon dried orange zest

1 teaspoon dried lemon zest

A FLORAL GARDEN PARTY

Sometimes, casual or impromptu get-togethers are the most fun because everyone feels comfortable and relaxed. I love eating in the garden when the weather gets warmer. The plants and flowers that start to bud this time of year are my first points of inspiration. I mix fragrant herbs with flowers for my tablescape and plan my menu from there, with light, bright, and refreshing flavors.

Hoja Santa-Wrapped Halibut with Lavender & Lemons

To blanch the hoja santa leaves: Fill a pot with water, add ¼ cup of salt and bring to a boil. Fill a large bowl halfway with ice water. Use a sharp knife to remove the thick part of the stem at the base of each leaf, making sure to leave the remainder of the spine of the leaf intact.

Using a slotted spoon, add one leaf at a time to the boiling water and blanch for 30 seconds until the leaf is pliable. Immediately remove from the boiling water and submerge in ice water. Repeat until all leaves are blanched and iced. Transfer the leaves to a sheet tray lined with a towel and lay flat. Use another towel to blot the leaves. Repeat this step until leaves are dry.

To wrap the halibut: On a clean cutting board, season all sides of the fish with salt, pepper, a sprinkle of chili flakes, and drizzle with olive oil. Lay a piece of halibut in the center of each leaf. Starting with the top and bottom of each leaf, neatly fold the edges of the leaves over the fish. Follow with the sides and wrap like a present.

On a clean work surface, lay out two lengths of string, approximately 1½ inches apart. Lay a wrapped piece of halibut across the strings, seam side up, so that the seam of the leaf is perpendicular to the strings. Top with a round of lemon and a sprig of lavender. Wrap twine and tie, taking care to secure the lemon round and lavender. Trim off any loose ends of twine. Repeat with the remaining halibut.

To cook: Heat oven to 400° F. Lay the wrapped halibut on a sheet tray lined with parchment and bake for 15 minutes. Serve with lemon wedges on the side.

INGREDIENTS

Serves 6

6 hoja santa leaves or parchment pouches

6 (6-ounce) pieces halibut, skinned & deboned

Salt & black pepper

Chili flakes

Olive oil

12 pieces butcher's twine, each cut 10" long

12 lemon rounds, cut ¼" thick

12 sprigs lavender, for garnish

2 lemons, cut into wedges, for garnish

Parting Gift | Garden Sea Salt

SUPPLIES

Makes 1 jar

½-ounce glass jar with cork top

¼ cup sea salt

1 teaspoon dried herbs (page 76)

(like rosemary, lavender, & thyme)

Additional dried spice or citrus

(like chili, garlic, lemon, & lime)

Waterproof stickers

You can sprinkle infused sea salts over practically anything. It's best used as a finishing salt or to season savory dishes, but you can also use it to rim a cocktail glass.

To make a jar of garden sea salt: Make sure herbs are completely dry before blending with salt. In a small bowl, combine the salt with the herbs and mix well. Add more herbs for a stronger infusion, or scale back to one part herbs to six parts salt, which will yield a milder flavor. If you are adding additional dried spices or citrus, add now.

Seal in an airtight jar with a sticker marking the date and instructions indicating that the infusion should sit for at least 3 weeks for the best flavor, and will keep for about a month afterwards.

Tips for the Table

Gather bundles of herbs and florals and tie with twine. Place into bowls down the center of the table to create deconstructed garlands.

—

As you prep, keep small bits of greens to decorate place settings. Anything works: flower petals and leaves, carrot tops, etc. Arrange into a wreath or tuck into a napkin.

—

When steaming fish in a leaf or parchment it continues to cook even after it comes out of the oven. Time your dish so that it's ready to enjoy as soon as you sit down.

—

Mix your glassware so that each place setting has a glass for both water and wine or a cocktail.

—

Simple votive candles give off nice, low, ambient lighting that makes any dinner feel intimate and special.

Spring Craft | Lavender Oil

SUPPLIES

Loose lavender, dried (page 76)

Mortar & pestle

Glass bottle with cork top

Lavender essential oil

Carrier oil

(like coconut, jojoba, or almond)

This lavender body oil is gentle, nourishing, and simple to make. Start with your favorite carrier oil—just make sure it has a mild, light scent so as to not overpower the aromatics. I love lavender for its ability to soothe the skin and calm the mind, but you can modify this in any way you like using your favorite herbs or flowers. Apply liberally after showering or bathing while skin is still damp.

To make a bottle of lavender oil: Cut dried lavender into small pieces and crush with a mortar and pestle. Place the herbs in a clean, dry jar and fill with carrier oil, taking care to cover the herbs by at least 1 inch. Add a few drops of essential oil. Stir well and seal. Place in direct sunlight, ideally on a windowsill, and shake gently once or more per day. Make sure to mark the day you make the oil and after four weeks, strain out the solids and keep the oil. To increase the strength of the scent, repeat this process or add 6 drops of essential oil per 1 ounce of infused oil.

Spring Craft | Dried Herbs

I love to dry my own herbs for aromatics, arrangements, or to have on hand to add flavor to a meal. My favorites are sage, thyme, rosemary, oregano, basil, mint, and lemon verbena, but you can use this method for any herbs you like.

To dry herbs: Carefully rinse each stem by washing in a bowl of cool water. Allow to air dry on a cooling rack or strainer, or gently blot with a soft towel. Weave twine through the stems, starting with the sturdiest one at the base and looping around the main stem. Leave a string trailing off at the end.

Hang the herbs upside down in a cool, dry room. You can find beautiful drying racks to hang from the ceiling or wall, or you can use the twine to wrap around a tack. Each day, inspect herbs for any signs of mold or bugs. If hanging against a wall, turn once a day. To avoid pests, wrap cheesecloth around your bundles and secure with twine. Once leaves are completely dry (anywhere from a few days to 1-2 weeks, depending on the moisture in the air), remove the dry leaves from the stems and place in a jar. Keep in a dark, dry cupboard.

SUPPLIES

Herbs of your choice

Twine

Cheesecloth

Scissors